GW01366903

Sun's
Hot,
Sea's
Cold

Paul Humphrey

Illustrated by
Sarah Young

Evans

4

…but it's cold in
the cave.

7

Our dog is hot...

8

...but this water is cold.

9

The rocks get hot in the sun...

10

...but it is still cool in the
rock pool.

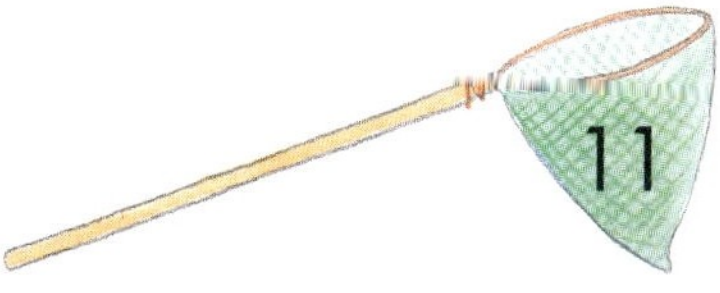

11

My lemonade
is cold.

My chips are hot.

14

  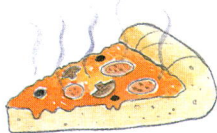 

My ice lolly is cold.

15

I have a bath in hot water...

16

...but I brush my teeth in cold water

17

It is hot in the desert...

…but cold at the North Pole.

It's hot in the rainforest...

…but cold on the
mountain top.

21

Crocodiles live where it is hot.

22

Penguins live where it is cold.

People live where it is hot...

...and people live where it is cold.

It is hot in the day...

...but it is cool at night.

I like it
when it's hot...

...and I like it when it's cold.

Goodbye!

Which of these things are hot or live where it is hot? Which things are cold or live where it is cold?